Little David, Play Your Harp

Little David,
Play Your Harp

Jodi Warren

Illustrations and Cover Design by Jodi Warren

Printed in the United States
Vivar Publishing

Dedication

This book is in dedication to my precious mother. She is now with the Lord, but her memory remains within my heart. The most intelligent and creative person I have ever known. She was always making a new song and worshipping the Lord in everything she would do. She is my example and inspiration.

I love you, Mom.
Psalm 100:2

Heartfelt thanks to my husband
who encourages me to aways do
what God has put on my heart.

And to my Lord,
who always gives me
ideas and thoughts in the night.
Job 35:10

TABLE OF CONTENTS

Foreword

With millions of written books dating back millennia, and thousands of titles on any one subject; what makes a book stand out and merit the investment of the time to read the text? In my opinion, it can often be the character of the author and the inspiration received in and through the writing.

In regard to Jodi, I can testify as no other. She is my precious wife of 36 years and the love of my life. In all my days, I have met very few who are so true and sincere. With all of her travels and vast life experiences, she still maintains the purity and wide-eyed excitement of a child. It is because of these things that I feel the Lord has chosen to inspire her and use her for His Holy works.

In "Little David, Play Your Harp", eternal truths are discovered by examining this legendary man's life. Flawed, yet still arguably one of this world's greatest Kings and a man after God's own heart. His legacy is found through the story of his amazing life and his writings within the Holy Bible. I pray as you read the words of this book, the Holy Spirit will shine light unto the truths presented and you find wisdom and encouragement in your own journey to become one whom the Lord loves and can call a child after His own heart.

— *Cory Warren*

Chapter 1

Have a Heart After God

For where your heart is,
there your treasure will be also.

Matthew 6:21

Looking on the life and story of David in the Bible, I came across many truths, thoughts, purposes and everyday life lessons that we can learn from his life. The Bible was divinely inspired by the Holy Spirit and God used men, like David to bring this inspiration to life, both in the Old and New Testaments. The story of David was not put in the Bible accidentally, but purposely. It's a purpose that many people will find inspirational to their personal lives.

As a shepherd, David foreshadows Christ. As we see, later in the New Testament where Jesus becomes and is known as the Good Shepherd. Have you ever wondered the reason why David was a man after God's heart? David was not recognized by man as a "special" individual that God would hand-pick. It seems to me that David picked God and then God picked David to use. David developed a heart and a desire for God. Each one of us have that choice and the availability to develop a heart after God, or not have a heart after God.

David at an early age chose God and chose to walk after his statutes and ways.   No matter what your age is – young or old – choose God and His ways. The bible says in Romans 10:9,

"If you confess with your mouth that Jesus is Lord and believe in your heart that God raised him from the dead, you will be saved."

There you have it, the first step – believe in Jesus.

David was the youngest of eight brothers. He was a shepherd and he tended the sheep. David's heart was after God wherever he was or in whatever he was doing. Throughout the bible you will find many songs that David wrote. God heard David's songs and loved them so much that He caused those songs to be placed in His Bible and we still get to hear them today.

Now let's get back to the matters of the heart. In Proverbs 4:23 it states,

> *"Keep your heart with all vigilance,*
> *for from it flow the springs of life."*

The heart is the center of feeling. It's where we are fearful, it's were we are anxious, and it's where we grieve. A heart can be hardened. A heart can be lightened. It's where we believe, ponder, sing, and meditate. That is why we need to hide God's word in our hearts. That is why we need to guard our hearts. That is also why we need to believe in our hearts that Christ has risen from the dead, so that we can be saved. We need to be like David and have a heart that yearns after God through not only words, but also through actions.

One of David's songs is found in the popular bible scripture, Psalm 23. It reads as follows:

> *"The Lord is my Shepherd; I shall not want.*
> *He maketh me to lie down in green pastures:*
> *he leadeth me beside the still waters. He*
> *restoreth my soul: he leadeth me in the paths*

of righteousness for his name's sake. Yea, though I walk through the valley of the shadow of death, I will fear no evil: for thou art with me; thy rod and thy staff they comfort me. Thou preparest a table before me in the presence of mine enemies: thou anointest my head with oil; my cup runneth over. Surely goodness and mercy shall follow me all the days of my life: and I will dwell in the house of the Lord for ever."

The 23rd Psalm has assisted me through many times in my life when I needed help. Those words were not only true back then, but are still just as true now. I find it interesting that while David was being afflicted, going astray, or being a King, his mind and thoughts went back to those things he had learned and experienced as a shepherd boy tending his sheep quietly out in the field. His thoughts took him back to his humble beginnings where God was training him for his future. We need to be content where God has us in each season of our lives. Our hearts need to be God focused and not focused on the things of this world.

I'm going to ask you a few questions here. *What's inside your heart? What are your motivations?* David's heart and motivation was to please God. This is one of the first things we learn from David. To have a heart set on pleasing God.

I wrote a song entitled *"What's Inside Your Heart"* years ago. It was one of the first songs that I ever wrote and the lyrics go like this:

"What's Inside Your Heart"

The heart it has much wickedness
it can cut, deceive, destroy.
Without the power of Jesus Christ
it can also be a toy.
Don't go by what you think
look to God above
and feel the peace of Christ
descend down like a dove.

What's inside your heart?
What's inside your mind?
What's the motivation for you to be kind?
Have you not love to give with nothing in return?
What rules in your life?
What's inside your heart?

Envy, jealousy, hatred, pride
these must never in you abide.
They will rob and steal your happiness
and take away all joy.
Fill your heart with words of life
that Jesus speaks of
and go out and show the world
that there really is Christ-like love.

What's inside your heart?
What's inside your mind?
What's the motivation for you to be kind?
Have you not love to give with nothing in return?
What rules in your life?
What's inside your heart?

Jodi Warren ©2017

We find that David's number one trait in pleasing God was to have a heart after God. It's a pretty simple truth, yet very profound and sometimes hard to find and maintain. We must continually overcome the world and steer our hearts to be after God.

The Lord
is my
Shepherd,
I shall not
want.

Chapter 2

Be Faithful in the Little Things

And we know that for those that love God, all things work together for good, for those who are called according to his purpose.

Romans 8:28

It seems evident that David was faithful in the little things. This led him to so much more in his life. David goes from being a shepherd boy to being the head of Saul's army, and then eventually becoming the King of Israel. In Luke 16:10 you will find the scripture,

> *"He that is faithful in that which is least is faithful also in much: and he that is unjust in the least is unjust in the much."*

Let's look back at David being faithful in the little things. We see that God was preparing David for his future. David is out in the field tending the sheep, minding his own business and out of the blue, he gets asked to play his harp for the King.

Now, King Saul had evil spirits troubling him. He told his advisors about this dilemma and they said he should get someone to play soothing music for him when he felt troubled. Saul tells his advisors to find him a skilled player of the harp. His advisors inform him that they have seen the son of Jesse play the harp skillfully and the Lord is with Him. The next thing you know, Saul sends a message to David's father (Jesse) asking him to send to him his son that plays the harp. David came and stood before Saul.   We read in 1 Samuel 16:23,

> *"And it came to pass when the evil spirit from God was upon Saul, that David took an harp, and played with his hand: so Saul*

*was refreshed, and was well, and the evil
spirit departed from him."*

He found favor with Saul and eventually became Saul's armor bearer. This is just how things tend to work in life. God knows the desire of your heart and wants to use you.

On one specific day when God chose to use him, he was asked by his father to take his brothers and the soldiers in the battlefield some food. The story of David and Goliath can be found in 1 Samuel 17.

It says that David arose early in the morning, left the sheep with a keeper and went as his father commanded him. When he got to the battleground, he left someone to keep watch over his carriage and ran into the army and came to his brothers and saluted them. He was talking with them and there came up the enemy's champion, the philistine named Goliath.

David heard the giant speaking and all of the other soldiers were so afraid of him that when they saw Goliath, they fled. David questioned, "Who is this uncircumcised Philistine that he should defy the armies of the living God?" He also asked the men beside him, "What will be done to the man that kills this Philistine?"

David's eldest brother heard this conversation and his anger was kindled against his brother. He asked David why he wasn't in the wilderness with the sheep? David's brother continued speaking and accused David of being filled with pride and arrogance and desiring to be the highest or best of them all. And David replied to him, "What have I done? Is there not a cause for me to be upset?" Others accused David of the same thing, when he was innocently sent there to bring his brothers food. They wrongly accused David, but he did not let that affect him. David continued doing what God had put on his heart.

Needless to say, if you are doing God's will in your life, sometimes you will face these types of obstacles. You may be wrongly accused, or even be told you shouldn't be there. The point we can learn from this is to not listen to others or even the lies that the devil puts in your heart, or on other men's hearts to hurt you, but do what God puts on your heart.

David was being faithful in his little things by being a courier and bringing food to the warriors on the frontline and now is put right smack dab in the middle of the Philistine battle. And now back to the story.

David says to them, "I will go and fight." Then Saul said "David, you can't fight, you are a youth and the Philistine, Goliath has been fighting since his youth – you will lose, you will die." David replies back to Saul and he tells him about the time when he kept the sheep and there came a lion and a bear, and they took a lamb out of the flock. He tells Saul, "I came out and struck the lion and then he came up against me and I caught him by his beard and struck and killed him. I have slain both a lion and a bear and the Lord delivered me out of the paw of the lion and the paw of the bear and He will deliver me out of the hand of this giant." Saul replies to David, "Go and the Lord be with thee." And the rest is history. David, with the help of God, slays Goliath with a sling and one stone.

David became a man of war after his battle with Goliath. He went from a young man, a shepherd in a field tending sheep, playing his harp quietly and peacefully, laying down by green pastures, to becoming a man of war, and then the King of Israel. His life shows us to be faithful in the little things.

If you feel discontent where God has you, be faithful. God will bring you to where He wants you to be if you are faithful, and if your heart is after the things of God, and you continue daily to fight the battle of faith in Christ Jesus.

Do not despise the little things, because in doing those little things you are living and learning. They lead to doing all the things that God has called you to do. Do what God puts on your heart. If it is meant to be, He will anoint it, and He will bless it. God will make it happen.

Chapter 3

God Looks at the Heart

For the Lord sees not as man sees:
man looks on the outward appearance,
God looks on the heart.

1 Samuel 16:7

In keeping with the story of David killing Goliath, we are going to look a little deeper into how he was able to do this task. How could a little shepherd boy kill a skilled champion giant? This is the question we are going to answer here in this chapter.

In trying to have David fight this fight the traditional way, King Saul equipped David with his own armor. Saul put a helmet of brass on David's head and covered him with a coat of mail. Then David went and got a sword and examined himself. He did not like all of that heavy armor. The helmet kept falling off of his head, he couldn't really see from side to side and it weighed him down. The heavy coat of mail made it impossible for him to run or move like he was used too. David said to Saul, "I can't go with these." He didn't like them so he took them off. He set down the sword, grabbed his shepherd's sling, went over to the brook and found five stones and put them in his shepherd's bag. He then took the sling in his hand and drew near to Goliath. Goliath saw David and was offended because he was a youth, ruddy, fair of countenance and did not look like the typical warrior. But little did Goliath know, that David was the ultimate warrior. He may not have appeared like it because he was not tall in stature or wearing the battle armor that was used in that day; however, David's heart was faithful after God. We are finding out that the answer to how David killed Goliath is a spiritual answer and not a physical one.

David had on his spiritual armor, which no one could see. It is the spiritual armor that pleases God. David had faith in his spiritual armor. This was all he needed, because his faith was in his God and he knew that God would come through for him. We find all we need to know about David's armor in Ephesians 6:10-18,

"Finally, be strong in the Lord and in the strength of his might. Put on the whole armor of God, that you may be able to stand against the schemes of the devil. For we do not wrestle against flesh and blood, but against the rulers, against the authorities, against the cosmic powers over this present darkness, against the spiritual forces of evil in the heavenly places. Therefore take up the whole armor of God, that you may be able to withstand in the evil day, and having done all, to stand firm. Stand therefore, having fastened on the belt of truth, and having put on the breastplate of righteousness, and, as shoes for your feet, having put on the readiness given by the gospel of peace. In all circumstances take up the shield of faith, with which you can extinguish all the flaming darts of the evil one; and take the helmet of salvation, and the sword of the Spirit, which is the word of God, praying at all times in the Spirit, with all prayer and supplication. To that end, keep alert with all perseverance, making supplication for all the saints."

Goliath said to David, "Am I a dog that you come to me with stones?" Then Goliath cursed at David by his gods and said to David, "Come to me and I will give your flesh to the birds of the air and the beasts of the field!"

David said back to Goliath, "You have come to me with a sword, spear and a shield, but I come to you in the name of the Lord of hosts and God of the armies of Israel, whom you have defiled. This day will the Lord deliver you into my hand and I will kill you and take your head from you and I will give the carcass of the host of the Philistine this day to the birds of the air and the wild beasts of the earth that all the earth may know that there is a God in Israel and all this assembly will know that the Lord did not need a sword and spear, because the battle is the Lords and He will give you into our hands."

With that, Goliath arose and drew close to meet David. David ran toward the army to meet the Philistine and put his hand in his shepherd's bag and took a stone and slung it.   The stone sank deep into Goliath's forehead and he fell upon his face to the earth. David killed the giant with only a sling and stone. And since there was no sword in David's hand, he ran and stood on Goliath, took Goliath's sword and drew it out of his sheath. He then cut off Goliaths head. When the philistines saw their champion was dead, they fled. David took Goliath's head and brought it to Jerusalem.

While men look at the outward appearance, God looks at the heart. We read in Acts 13:22, regarding how God looks at the heart, specifically David's heart;

"And when he had removed him (Saul), he raised up David to be their king, of whom he testified and said, 'I have found in David the son of Jesse a man after my heart, who will do all my will'."

If you take one thing away from this, always remember and don't forget – God looks at the heart.

Chapter 4

Watch Out for Your Enemies

Be sober-minded; Be watchful.
Your adversary the devil prowls like a
roaring lion, seeking someone to devour.

1 Peter 5:8

Life was not meant to be easy. You will have much trouble in this world, but God has overcome. This life is actually a proving ground for our faith in Christ Jesus. We all will face obstacles. Even Jesus faced obstacles while he was here and walked the earth. He was tempted, but he did not sin. Jesus is our perfect example. David just may be our perfectly imperfect example. An example of what to do, and what not to do. In this case, David's example is what to do with your enemies.

Saul eventually became jealous of David. He was offended that the people praised David instead of him, saying, "Saul has slain his thousands and David his ten thousands." Those words from the people made Saul be jealous of him from that day forward. An evil spirit would come on Saul from time to time and make him want to kill David. This forced David to hide from Saul on numerous occasions. Saul was afraid of David because David had the Spirit of God on him, so Saul removed him from his presence. All of Israel and Judah loved David.

In Psalm 59, David writes about praying for deliverance from his enemies. David proclaimed that God was his strength and would watch over him.

Throughout the life of David, we find him repeatedly running from his enemies. David at one time even had to pretend he was insane before the King of Gath, so he could escape from Saul and his men. During this time of tribulation in David's life, we find so many of our favorite passages in the book of Psalms. It's sometimes in our valleys, where we get to experience the presence of the Lord powerfully.

There were two times when David had the chance to kill Saul, but did not. In the first instance, David was in the Desert of En Gedi and Saul took three thousand able men from Israel to set out and look for David near the Crags of the wild goats. They came to a cave and Saul went in, not knowing that David and his men were already in the cave. David crept up unnoticed and cut off a corner of Sauls robe instead of taking his life. Then in 1 Samuel 26 he could have speared Saul to the ground, but did not. This time however, Saul heard David's voice and said to him, "Is that your voice, David my son?" David replied, "Yes, and why are you pursuing your servant? What wrong have I done and what am I guilty of?"

Saul realizes that he sinned and apologizes to David. He asked David to come back because he had considered his life precious and promised not to harm him again. He said, "Surely, I have acted like a fool and have done wrong." He further said, "May you be blessed, you will do great things and surely triumph."

David returned to the land of the Philistines, but began to think to himself that one of these days he would be destroyed by the hand of Saul. That thought was a constant concern for David, so he decided to move to Ziglag. When Saul heard that David had moved to Ziglag, he stopped pursing David and left him alone.

Sometimes we go through things that help us grow and become who we are called to be. God also tests our hearts through other people and circumstances that come into our lives. We must always remember that God is for us and not against us. God will deliver.

Our main enemy according to 1 Peter 5:8 is the devil. He's running to and fro like a roaring lion, looking for someone to devour, a life to destroy. We need to be ready to take on that giant. We need to always be prepared for our spiritual battles and our physical battles.

We must be like David during these times. We must do what is right and fully rely on God. He will provide the lamb. God will provide that person to help. He will provide that wisdom for the next step we must take. God will meet our needs according to His riches in glory.

These are the times when our faith can be proven, our love for the Lord can shine and God's love for us can be shown. Sometimes our enemies can actually lead us to our destiny. God is excited to prepare a table before us in the presence our enemies if we will just let Him.

And he shall be
like a tree planted
by the rivers
of water,

that bringeth
forth his fruit in
his season;

his leaf also
shall not wither;
and whatsoever
he doeth
shall prosper.

Psalm 1:3

Chapter 5

Always Have a Song

He put a new song in my mouth,
a song of praise to our God.

Psalm 40:3

There are many places in the Bible where David sang or danced before the Lord. In 2 Samuel 6:14 we read that David danced before the Lord with all his might while bringing the ark of the covenant to Jerusalem, letting all see his full devotion to God through movement and song. David always had a song in his heart and didn't let the weight of the world bring him down. In Psalm 108:1-2 David says,

> *"My heart is steadfast, O God! I will sing and make melody with all my being! Awake, O Harp and lyre! I will awake the dawn!"*

The secret words here are "My heart is steadfast." It's that place within your spirit and within your heart, where you reach and touch God. It's the place where God, who is looking throughout the earth to find those who are faithful, and He sees you. Your heart becomes fixed on Him, that it makes Him stop and listen, and you have His attention.

Not only with dance and song did David praise the Lord, but also with harps, cymbals, tambourines and all other kinds of instruments. Play your instrument. Use your voice. Honor the Lord with all that He has given you. David says in Psalm 89:1,

> *"I will sing of the steadfast love of the Lord forever; with my mouth I will make known   your   faithfulness   to   all generations."*

One of the first scriptures I decided to memorize in the bible was Psalm 34:1-8;

"I will bless the Lord at all times: his praise shall continually be in my mouth. My soul makes its boast in the Lord; let the humble hear and be glad. Oh, magnify the LORD with me, and let us exalt his name together! I sought the LORD, and he answered me and delivered me from all my fears. Those who look to him are radiant, and their faces shall never be ashamed. This poor man cried, and the Lord heard him and saved him out of all his troubles. The angel of the Lord encamps around those who fear him, and delivers them. Oh, taste and see that the Lord is good! Blessed is the man who takes refuge in him!"

What a handful of advice and wisdom from the heart of David. Having God's praise in our mouths continually will settle a lot of arguments here on this earth. We should be so busy being in love with Jesus and singing His praises that the problems of this world can't bring us down.

Another way to have a song in your heart is to give. It's better to give than to receive. Giving is a response to the song that God puts within your heart. True joy comes from putting Jesus first, others second and yourself last (J-

O-Y). You can give through the use of your gifts. You can give through your time. You can give to others through the abundance of your blessings. Your song is not just in musical lyrics or sounds, but also in the way you conduct yourself in the area of giving. A way of giving can be as simple as kind words or a smile to someone.

You might think, "How can I keep a song in my heart?" One answer to that question is to allow the Holy Spirit to move in your heart. It is the Spirit's wind that will bring the song to your heart. You will begin living the way God wants you to and not even know it, all because you allowed the Holy Spirit to fill you and make you new. You'll be singing a song in your heart and think, "I didn't know I even knew that song." That's what the Holy Spirit does; He moves in ways we don't understand.

Begin now to sing a new song and to bless the Lord at all times. Let His praise continually be in your mouth. No matter what you are going through remember to have a song or find a song in the midst of it all!

He leads me beside
the still waters!

Chapter 6

Give Thanks to the Lord

The Lord is my strength and my shield;
in him my heart trusts and I am helped.
My heart rejoices and I will give thanks to him.

Psalm 28:7

As we read the many chapters and scriptures based on the life of David, we find a place where David writes a psalm of gratitude. Let's read what the prophet Samuel expressed from this passage in 1 Chronicles 16:7-11. These verses are about David giving thanks to the Lord.

> *"Then on that day David first appointed that thanksgiving be sung to the Lord by Asaph and his brothers. Oh give thanks to the Lord; call upon his name; make known his deeds among the peoples! Sing to him, sing praises to him; tell of all his wondrous works! Glory in his holy name; let the hearts of those who seek the Lord rejoice! Seek the Lord and his strength; seek his presence continually!"*

Gratitude is another attribute David held onto. David had gratitude for the Lord. He said to give thanks to the Lord, call upon His name, and make known His deeds among the people. Not only by singing to Him, but also seeking His face continually, and meditating on His word day and night.

Gratitude in short is being thankful for all that the Lord has done. David showed his gratitude to God in his good times, in his bad times, in his times of plenty and even in his times of correction. Be thankful you have a Heavenly Father that loves you. No matter what you have done or what you need to do, where you are at or where you have been, your Heavenly Father loves you. The things He presents to you are for your good.

When you read about David's life, you read about him killing a bear and a lion, slaying a giant, becoming King of Israel, slaughtering tens of thousands, and winning battles. On the other hand, we also read about David running from Saul, his adultery with Bathsheba, and other things that were not holy nor honored God or the Holy Spirit. However, David's heart and ways constantly led him back to repentance and gratitude for God.

Looking a little deeper into 1 Chronicles 16:7 we find that this is where David celebrates God's mercy and God's marvelous deeds. David gave burnt offerings and peace offerings before God. Now in our day we are to offer a sacrifice of praise to the Lord and also our own lives as a living sacrifice. In Hebrews 13:15 we read,

"Through him then let us continually offer
up a sacrifice of praise to God, that is the
fruit of lips that acknowledge his name."

David was thankful to God for everything that He took him through and brought him through. He never took anything for granted. Psalm 100:4 says,

"Enter his gates with thanksgiving, and his
courts with praise! Give thanks to him; bless
his name!"

We do not have to burn sacrifices of lambs anymore. Jesus became the Lamb of God. He is the one and only sacrifice. We get to give our sacrifices in the form of praise, time, worship and to burn the midnight oil of prayer. We get to present our bodies as a living sacrifice, holy and acceptable unto God, which is our reasonable service. I don't know about you, but I'm grateful for that. I don't know what I'd do if I had to go out and pick a little spotless lamb and put it on an altar. That's what they had to do. But we get to praise, we get to worship, we get to live holy lives, all because of Jesus, our Good Shepherd, who became the spotless Lamb of God.

We have been given so much in this day and age. We have a lot to be accountable for. Let our hearts rejoice. Let our hearts worship the Lord in His beauty of holiness, just like David did. We need to say in our hearts as David did, save us, O God of our salvation. Gather us together and deliver us that we may give thanks to your Holy name and glory in your praise. Let's give thanks to the Lord because He is good and His mercy endures forever!

Chapter 7

Fight the Battle

I can do all things through him who
strengthens me.

Philippians 4:16

Fight the good fight of faith. We must fight to win our battles. David did, as we see in the battle between David and Goliath. David came to the battlefield as a food delivery person, and when he arrived, he heard things that made his soul upset. They were talking badly about his Lord and his Saviour. However, David didn't just stand there, he decided to do something about it. If David did not take that stand for his faith, the battle would have been won by the Philistines. Things might be different today had not little David decided to take a stand. Sometimes it takes just one person.

You might think, "What can I do in this situation? I am just one person and not really part of it all." David is our example to fight and do what God puts on our hearts. We must pick up those five little stones. Your words and thoughts matter, especially when they are on the side of righteousness. One person can put a thousand to flight as we see in Joshua 23:10,

> *"One man of you puts to flight a thousand, since it is the Lord your God who fights for you, just as he promised you."*

It references this again, in Deuteronomy 32:30-31 within the song of Moses,

> *"How could one have chased a thousand, and two have put ten thousand to flight, unless their Rock had sold them, and for the Lord*

had given them up? For their rock is not as
our Rock; our enemies are by themselves."

Meaning that one singular person can defeat many, and do great things with faith in the Lord and help from the Lord. David did it. He had faith that the Lord would come through for him and look what his faith did. The Lord was his Rock.

The battle belongs to the Lord. Your battle belongs to the Lord. Let's read how David's battle belonged to the Lord in I Samuel 17:47,

> *"And all this assembly may know that the*
> *Lord saves not with the sword and spear.*
> *For the battle is the Lord's and he will give*
> *you into our hand."*

Then we go to verse 48 and it says,

> *"When the Philistine arose and came and*
> *drew near to meet David, David ran quickly*
> *toward the battle line to meet the Philistine."*

And we continue to verse 49 and 50,

> *"And David put his hand in his bag and*
> *took out a stone and slung it and struck*
> *the Philistine on his forehead. The stone*
> *sank into his forehead, and he fell on his*
> *face to the ground. So David prevailed*

over the Philistine with a sling and with a stone, and struck the Philistine and killed him. There was no sword in the hand of David."

David's victory was not by might, nor by power, but by his faith in God, which had already been tested and proven in his life. I think we can bring this into our lives with the scripture, Zechariah 4:6

"Not by might, nor by power, but by my Spirit, says the Lord of hosts."

Some battles aren't fought in the physical realm, but are fought in the spiritual realm. The stones we can use to fight our battles are prayer, fasting, believing, having faith, and trusting in God and His holy words. Pick up your stone of prayer and fling it. Pick up your stone of faith and throw it. Start quoting scriptures over your battle. Those are just some of the stones that God has for us to use, and then let Him do the rest.

Years ago, I was watching the "Sound of Music" and it came to the part where the Von Trapp family had to flee from the Nazis. The nun said to Maria, "You will not be alone, remember to lift your eyes up to the hills from whence cometh your help." Those words she said to Maria stayed with me for days and from that beautiful truth came the song, *"Forever."* The lyrics are as follows.

"Forever"

You see me, You hear me,
You love me, You're near me,
All my life is in Your hands.
You save me, You keep me,
You shade me, You lead me,
All my days you have planned.

I will call upon Your name,
Lift my eyes to a higher plain,
My help comes from You.
And I know I will not fail,
Cause I know that You are there,
Your hand covers me.
Forever.

You hold me, embrace me,
You guide me, You place me,
All I am you have made.
You shield me, You lift me,
You comfort, You heal me,
Every day, in all my ways.

So, I will call upon Your name,
Lift my eyes to a higher plain,
My help comes from You.
And I know I will not fail,
Cause I know that You are there,
Your hand covers me.
Forever.

Jodi Warren ©2017

What the nun said to Maria that day is also found in Psalm 121:1, which reads like this,

> *"I lift my eyes to the hills. From where*
> *does my help come?"*

And if we continue on to read in verse 2 it says,

> *"My help comes from the Lord who made*
> *heaven and earth."*

God's words are alive! Pick up your stones, stand your ground and fight your battle with the help of the Lord!

Chapter 8

Don't Become Distracted

Do not swerve from the right or the left;
turn your feet away from evil

Proverbs 4: 27

In the areas of faith and trusting in the Lord, we see David being an excellent example for us to follow, however, in other areas David was not the perfect role model. I think that is why God uses David so much in the Bible as an example for us. Jesus was the Good Shepherd and He had no sin. He is our perfect example and had to be so that he could become the Lamb of God. David was a Shepherd, but his life was filled with areas of sin. No one is perfect. If you are then cast the first stone. Jesus said in, John 8:7,

> *"Let him who is without sin among you be the first to throw a stone at her."*

David's life is such a good example for us to follow in *almost* every area. He did have times of sin. However, what made him succeed and remain with a heart after God is that he always repented and asked God for forgiveness. Let's read about one of David's distractions. Her name was Bathsheba. This story is found in 2 Samuel 11:1-5,

> "In the spring of the year, the time when kings go out to battle, David sent Joah, and his servants with him, and all Israel. And they ravaged the Ammonites and besieged Rabbah. But David remained in Jerusalem. It happened, late one afternoon, when David arose from his couch and was walking on the roof of the King's house, that he saw from the roof a woman bathing; and the woman

was very beautiful. And David sent and inquired about the woman. And one said, "Is not this Bathsheba, the daughter of Eliam, the wife of Uriah the Hittite?" So David sent messengers and took her, and she came to him and he lay with her. Then she returned to her house. And the woman conceived, and she sent and told David, "I am with child."

This distraction should have never happened. But it did and David had to devise a plan so he couldn't be blamed for this. He crafted a plan, a plan of murder. He sent her husband off to the front lines of battle where he was killed. Problem solved, but not in God's eyes. Be sure your sins will find you out. David and Bathsheba's baby died. This tragedy broke David's heart. However, David's heart was after God and this is where the psalm, "Create in me a clean heart" arose. We read his prayer of repentance in Psalm 51:10-12,

> *"Create in me a clean heart O God, and renew a right spirit within me. Cast me now away from thy presence; and take not your Holy Spirit from me. Restore to me the joy of your salvation and uphold me with a willing spirit."*

In these verses David repented. Showing to us that only God can make us a new creation. Only God can restore us. God forgave David. David's heart led him to repent and turn the needed 180° away from sin and towards God. Watch out for the devil in your life, as he is out to kill, steal and destroy. The things of this world will pass away, but God's word does not. Only what is done for Jesus will last.

Years ago, I wrote a song entitled, *"Only What's Done for Christ Will Last."* The lyrics are as follows:

"Only What's Done for Christ"

You may have riches or not a thing,
may be a pauper or may be a king.
The grass it withers and the flowers they fade;
Eternal life is the gift He gave.

Boy does life ever go by fast,
one day you're ten and then twenty years pass.
It took some time for me to learn this fact and that's
only what' done for Christ will last.

Someday we'll meet him up in the sky,
where we'll be changed in the blink of an eye.
I know for certain deep within my heart,
When I see Jesus, He says I did my part.

Boy does life ever go by fast,
one day you're ten and then twenty years pass.
It took some time for me to learn this fact and that's
only what' done for Christ will last.

Jodi Warren ©2017

Don't become distracted by things of this world, as the things of this world are all temporary. What God has called you to do, is way more important than anything this world has to offer. The things of this world may make you feel good temporarily, but God and His holy words are eternal. It says in Matthew 6:19-21,

"Do not lay up for yourselves treasure on earth, where moth and rust destroy and where thieves break in and steal, but lay up for yourselves treasures in heaven, where neither moth nor rust destroys and where thieves do not break in and steal. For where your treasure is, there your heart will be also."

We see once again it all goes back to the heart. Don't become distracted by the things of this world! Only what's done for Christ will stand the test of time. Set your heart on the things above.

I am the Good Shepherd

Chapter 9

Be Filled with The Spirit

But you will receive power when the Holy Spirit has come upon you, and you will be my witnesses in Jerusalem, and in Judea and Samaria, and to the end of the earth.

Acts 1:8

In 1 Samuel 16:13, we find that the prophet Samuel anoints David as the next king and the Spirit of God immediately comes upon David at that time.

"And the Spirit of the Lord rushed upon David from that day forward."

This shows us that David was chosen by God and empowered by the Holy Spirit to fulfill his role as king.

We need to have such an unforgettable moment in our lives. A time that we remember where a change happened. I have heard it said before that it's a time where our name gets changed. For Paul in the New Testament, it was when God changed his name from Saul to Paul. For Jacob, in the Old Testament, it was where his name was changed from Jacob to Israel. For David, it was when Samuel anointed him as the next King.

I remember the moment I was filled with the Holy Spirit. It was at the age of eleven on a summer night when I attended a children's church service. There were about 300 children in attendance and the service was about being filled with the Holy Spirit. It was on that night that I chose to walk deeper with God. I had already accepted Him as my Lord and Saviour at an earlier age, but was being drawn closer. I remember sitting in my seat and the Holy Spirit was dealing with my heart. They announced to the congregation that if anyone wanted to receive the Holy Spirit they should come forward, so I did. I made that walk of faith. After some moments of prayer, they invited anyone who made this commitment to come over to the side room where they could speak with us and answer any of our questions. Well, I was actually disappointed because nothing really happened. I didn't feel anything.

I went home that night praying in my heart and letting God know I wanted Him and His fulness. It wasn't until the next day when I was laying on the bottom bunk bed in our room, praying and talking with God that something amazing happened. I don't know where my other family members were or what they were doing. I just remember that my hands went up while I laid there on that bottom bunk and I began speaking in an unknown tongue. I remember my hands and arms feeling so light and I felt the overwhelming presence of the Lord. No one was around. It was just me, the quiet of the room and the presence of the Holy Spirit. This was that memorable moment for me. The moment that I will never forget nor deny. I know that I was filled with the Holy Spirit. God's beautiful gift was given to me. It's the moment that I was, without a doubt, forever changed.

Even after David sinned, we see in Psalm 51 where he went on to say, "Take not thy Holy Spirit from me. Restore unto me the joy of thy salvation and renew a right spirit within me." David knew the importance of God's presence, God's Spirit, God's anointing. He didn't want the Holy Spirit taken from him.

One of my favorite verses in the Bible is found in Psalm 139:7-12, and it says,

> *"Where shall I go from your Spirit? Or where shall I flee from your presence? If I ascend to heaven, you are there! If I make my bed in Sheol, you are there! If I take the wings of the morning and dwell in the uttermost parts of the sea, even there your hand shall lead me and your right hand shall hold me. If I say, Surely the darkness shall cover me, and the light about me be night, even the darkness is not dark to you; the night is bright as the day for darkness is as light with you."*

God's presence is so important. With Him, all things are possible and I can do all things, because He strengthens me.

In Ephesians 5:18, it says to be filled with the Spirit. You might say, how can I know if someone is or if I am filled with the Spirit? One of the ways is to look at their life. The Bible says that you will know them by their fruit. The Fruit of the Spirit is found in Galatians 5:22-23,

> *"But the fruit of the Spirit is love, joy, peace, patience, kindness, goodness, faithfulness, gentleness, self-control; against such things is no law."*

David was filled with the Holy Spirit when Samuel anointed him as the future King of Israel. Allow the Holy Spirit to move in your life. The Holy Spirit moves in ways we don't understand. It is the Spirit's wind that will bring the answers to your heart. You will begin living the way God wants you to and not even know it, all because you allowed the Holy Spirit to fill you and make you new.

The final words that Jesus spoke to his disciples before he ascended into heaven are found in Acts 1:4-5,

> *"And while staying with them he ordered them not to depart from Jerusalem, but to wait for the promise of the Father, which, he said, "you heard from me; for John baptized with water, but you will be baptized with the Holy Spirit not many days from now."*

We then continue on to read in Acts 1:7-8

> *He said to them, "It is not for you to know times or seasons that the Father has fixed by his own authority, but you will receive power when the Holy Spirit has come upon you, and you will be my witnesses in Jerusalem and in all Judea and Samaria, and to the end of the earth."*

As we remain in the book of Acts, we come to the powerful 2nd chapter of Acts where we find that there came a sound like a mighty rushing wind and they were all filled with the Spirit.

The book of Acts is one of my favorite books in the Bible. It was written by Luke who also wrote the gospel of Luke. The book of Acts as well contains many splendid occurrences that have taken my faith to the next level and that I find so interesting to learn and read about.

In Acts 2:25 Luke repeats the words of David,

> *"I saw the Lord always before me, for he is at my right hand that I may not be shaken; therefore, my heart was glad, and my tongue rejoiced; my flesh also will dwell in hope. For you will not abandon my soul to Hades, or let your Holy One see corruption. You have made known to me the paths of life; you will make me full of gladness with your presence."*

And then Luke continues to write about David beginning in verse 29;

> *"Brothers, I may say to you with confidence about the patriarch David that he both died and was buried, and his tomb is with us to this day. Being therefore a prophet, and knowing that God had sworn with an oath to him that he would set one of his descendants on his throne, he foresaw and spoke about the resurrection of the Christ, that he was not abandoned to Hades, nor did his flesh see corruption. This Jesus God raised up, and of that we all are witnesses. Being therefore exalted at the right hand of God,*

and having received from the Father the promise of the Holy Spirit, he has poured out this that you yourselves are seeing and hearing. For David did not ascend into the heavens, but he himself says, 'The Lord said to my right hand, until I make your enemies your footstool."

We find that being filled with the Spirit is another example David's life gives to us. David knew that with the help of his Almighty Lord and the Holy Spirit, he could do anything. We can have that too.

God gave us the Holy Spirit to be our power, our wisdom, our comforter, to give us understanding, to give us the fear of the Lord, to be that little small voice to know what is right and what is wrong. All we need to do is listen and obey.

I treasure God's presence and His Holy Spirit. They have taken me through many of my life's challenges, tribulations, and battles. I challenge you to be filled with the Holy Spirit.

Chapter 10

Keep God's Commandments

If you love me,
you will keep my commandments.

John 14:15

Throughout the writings of David, we find him saying how he loves to keep Gods ways, laws and statutes. Psalms 18:22 reads,

> *"For all his rules were before me, and his statutes I did not put away from me."*

Psalm 105:45 says,

> *"That they might keep his statutes, and observe his laws. Praise the Lord."*

In 1 Kings 2:1-4, we find David's final advice to his son Solomon (who was anointed the next King of Israel). His advice went like this,

> *"When David's time to die drew near, he commanded Solomon his son saying, 'I am about to go the way of all the earth. Be strong, and show yourself a man, and keep the charge of the Lord your God, walking in his ways and keeping his statutes, his commandments, his rules and his testimonies, as it is written in the Law of Moses, that you may prosper in all that you do and wherever you turn, that the Lord may establish his word that he spoke concerning me saying, 'If your sons pay close attention to their way, to walk before me in*

faithfulness with all their heart and with all their soul, you shall not lack a man on the throne of Israel.'"

Those verses can sum a lot of things up. We need to walk in the ways of the Lord and to keep His commandments. David learned so much in his lifetime, through his pain, through his successes, through his suffering, and through his blessings. Through all of this David says over and over again to keep Gods statues and ways. Psalm 119:5 says,

"Oh that my ways may be steadfast in keeping your statutes!"

Let's look at the law of Moses and the Ten Commandments. They can be found in Exodus 20 and they are as follows,

1. Thou shalt not have no other gods before me.
2. Thou shalt not make unto thee any graven image.
3. Thou shalt not take the name of the Lord thy God in vain.
4. Thou shalt remember the Sabbath and keep it holy.
5. Honor thy father and mother.
6. Thou shalt not kill.
7. Thou shalt not commit adultery.
8. Thou shalt not steal.
9. Thou shalt not bear false witness.
10. Thou shalt not covet.

These are the commandments that David stood by and tried to follow. Sometimes with success and sometimes not, but he always had a repentant heart. A heart that turned his eyes to the Lord as he asked for forgiveness when he did wrong.

In the New Testament, Jesus becomes the Lamb of God. He then gives us the two greatest commandments and they are found in Matthew 22:37-40. Jesus was asked which is the greatest commandment in the law and He replied,

"You shall love the Lord your God with all your heart and with all your soul and with all your mind. This is the great and first commandment. And a second is like it: You shall love your neighbor as yourself. On these two commandments depend all the Law and the Prophets."

If we love the Lord with all our hearts, then the Ten Commandments become easy to keep. We would never want to do anything that would dishonor our Lord. Don't focus on the what not to do, instead focus on the what to do and that is to love. Love the Lord with all your heart and love your neighbor as yourself and the rest will all fall into place. David wrote in Psalm 119:12,

"Blessed art you, O Lord: teach me your statutes!"

We find that wanting to and trying to keep God's commandments and ways are how David maintained a heart after God. We should always try to follow God's way and will for our lives. We need to ask God repeatedly for the grace we need to follow His ways. We read in Psalm 119:10-11,

> "With my whole heart I seek you; let me not wander from your commandments! I have stored up your word in my heart, that I might not sin against you!"

Let me ask you, are you reading God's word? Are you hiding His word in your heart? In Psalm 119:33-35 it states,

> "Teach me, O Lord, the way of your statutes; and I will keep it unto the end. Give me understanding, that I may keep your law and observe it with my whole heart. Lead me in the path of your commandments, for I delight in it."

And David goes on to speak of God's ways in Psalm 119:47-48,

> "For I find my delight in your commandments, which I love. I will lift up my hands toward your commandments, which I love, and I will meditate on your statutes."

If we seek the Lord, He will find us. David constantly sought after the Lord. He continually kept Gods commandments and feared the Lord. God desires to protect us and to give victory to His faithful children.

As we read David's psalms, we can keep reading scripture after scripture about meditating on God's word, keeping God's laws, statutes, and ways. We need to love God's laws and ways, keep them, and meditate on them.

Chapter 11

Have a Humble Heart

Humility is the fear of the Lord;
its wages are riches, honor and life.

Proverbs 22:4

David's humility made him a great leader, a great person, and a beautiful servant. He was anointed King, yet he still wanted to live the simple life of a shepherd. He killed the giant, he slew tens of thousands, and yet he kept himself a good follower to whom God had placed as King. He could've killed Saul two times and taken his place easily, yet he refrained because he wanted to honor God's words. He was a gifted musician and played before the King, yet he still wanted to quietly tend the sheep. His gifts did not make his heart proud. David only wanted to please God. David had a servant's heart. We see that this is another parallel that David had to Jesus. David was a servant and Jesus was the Servant King.

Not only was David humble, but he was also honest. He knew when he made a mistake and would confess to God. He was honest with God and honest with himself. If we are honest with ourselves, we know that without the Lord we are nothing. Without the Holy Spirit, without God's wisdom, without God's truth, without God Himself we can do nothing. All the glory goes to the Lord, because that is where our help comes from. In Psalm 10:12, we read,

> *"Arise, O Lord; O God, lift up thine hand: forget not the humble."*

And in Psalm 10:17 it states,

> *"O Lord, you hear the desire of the afflicted; you will strengthen their heart; you will incline your ear."*

You can tell in David's writings that he had a high view of his Lord and he knew that God was his reason for living, his reason for success, and his reason to worship and praise.

The humble will submit to God's word and will commit to keeping God's commandments. David delighted in keeping God's words and ways. David knew he had shortcomings, so he was not filled with pride. He knew that his strength was in the Lord. He delighted in submitting to God. David always gave God the victory. In 2 Samuel 22:22-23,

> *"For I have kept the ways of the Lord and have not wickedly departed from my God. For all his rules were before me, and from his statutes I did not turn aside."*

David knew that his strength and successes all came from the Lord. We read in Psalm 18:29-36,

> *" For by you I can run against a troop and by my God I can leap over a wall. This God-his way is perfect; the word of the Lord proves true; he is a shield for all those who take refuge in him. For who is God, but the Lord? And who is a rock, except our God? The God who equipped me with strength and made my way blameless. He made my feet like the deer and set me secure on the heights. He trains my hands for war, so that my arms can bend a bow of bronze. You have given me a*

shield of your salvation, and your right hand supported me, and your gentleness made me great. You gave a wide place for my steps under me, and my feet did not slip."

The humble will obey God's word. David delighted in obeying Gods word. Over and over again you will read David saying how he meditates on God's word. An example of this is found in Psalm 1:2, which reads,

"But his delight is in the law of the Lord, and on his law he meditates day and night."

David submitted to God's will and he never tried to be more than he was. He knew his weaknesses. When David was weak, God was strong and David knew that. Looking back to Psalm 23, David states,

"I shall not want."

David was in want of nothing that the world had to offer. His desire was God's peace, God's placement, God's restoration, God's vengeance, and God's righteousness.

Being humble is not about walking around with your head down. It's about walking around with your head up knowing that you are a child of God, walking in His ways, and obeying His statutes.

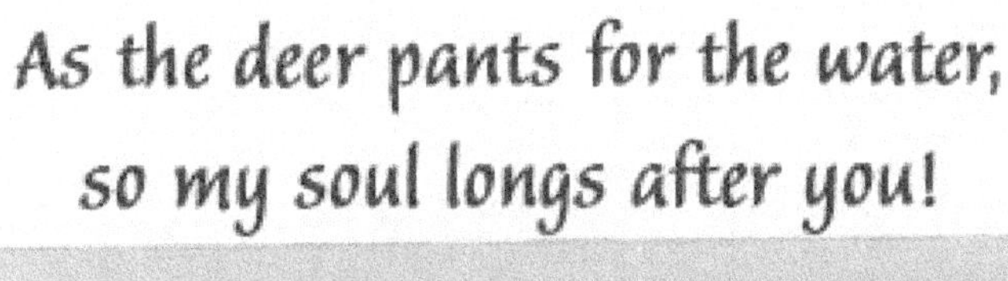
As the deer pants for the water,
so my soul longs after you!

Chapter 12

Meditate on God's Words

I will meditate on your precepts,
and fix my eyes on your ways.

Psalm 119:15

Another word that we read about many times in David's life and Psalms is the word, "meditate." The meaning of meditate in God's word is to think deeply on what God is saying. One of the behaviors a Christian can adopt to meditate on God's word is to pray. Paul, in the Bible tells us in 1 Thessalonians 5:17,

"Pray without ceasing"

After reading much of David's writings, it seems as if he always did have a prayer in his heart. It seemed like he always had his mind focused on the things of God. You might think, "It's impossible to pray all the time." If you love the Lord and your heart is focused on Him in all of your daily life's actions, you just may be praying without ceasing, without even knowing it.

Other ways to meditate as a Christian are to read and study God's word. Paul also says in 2 Timothy 2:15,

> *"Do your best to present yourself to God as one approved, a worker who has no need to be ashamed, rightly handling the word of truth."*

We can also memorize God's word. We need to hide God's word in our hearts. David certainly had God's words hidden in his heart. He tells us so in Psalm 119:11,

"Thy word have I hid in my heart, that I might not sin against Thee."

By doing these few little things that God instructs us to do we are strengthening ourselves. We are making ourselves better people. We are becoming who God wants us to be. We are and will become more like Jesus, which is our ultimate and final goal in this life. David writes in Psalm 63:6-8,

"When I remember you upon my bed, and meditate on you in the watches of the night; for you have been my help, and in the shadow of your wings I will sing for joy. My soul clings to you; your hand upholds me."

While David sleeps in the night, his soul follows the Lord and he meditates on God. I feel that sometimes in our sleep the Lord will speak to us and can really see our hearts. I love the mornings when I wake up after having had an interesting dream and I did the right thing in my dream. I'm always hoping to wake up to a song that the Lord put on my heart in the night. In Psalm 42:8, David says,

"By day the Lord commands his steadfast love, and at night his song is with me, a prayer to the God of my life."

One of the songs I've written comes to mind as I write this entitled, *"Saviour, Redeemer, Friend,"* and it goes like this,

"Saviour, Redeemer, Friend"

When I wake up in the morning
What will this day hold?
Will it bring me blessing
or will troubles unfold?
All of this worry that I feel inside
doesn't do any good
when I know He will provide.

He sees me, He hears me,
He knows my every care
and He's watching, waiting,
to let me know He's there.
No matter what tomorrow holds,
I know He knows my name,
My Saviour, Redeemer, Friend.

As I lay my head down to sleep
I hear Him say to me
Words of life and happiness
and He's set me free.
I close my eyes, I go to sleep
the victory is mine
knowing that He will prove
He's been there all the time.

Saviour, blessed Saviour
Help me through this trial.
Redeemer, loving Redeemer
Be with me all the while.

He sees me, He hears me,
He knows my every care
and He's watching, waiting,
to let me know He's there.
No matter what tomorrow holds,
I know He knows my name,
My Saviour, Redeemer, Friend.

Jodi Warren ©2017

The bible frequently speaks about David meditating on God's words. The more I am alive in this world, the more I realize how important it is to meditate on God's holy words. When you do that, you will have a song in your heart. God's words are alive and they become songs, they become phrases, they become feelings that your insides just can't stop repeating and you can rely on. God's words will not return void. What is so overwhelming is that David, who didn't have the completed Bible, was making those words for us. Now all we have to do is read them, meditate on them and it becomes a song in our hearts too.

We need to be with the Lord so much during the day that His songs are with us in the night. God wants to give you rest, He wants to give you peace, He wants you to succeed. Don't give the devil room in your life. Begin your journey to be more like Jesus by meditating on His words.

Chapter 13

David & Jesus

Many are the plans in the mind of a man,
but it is the purpose of the Lord that will stand.

Proverbs 19:21

Throughout the Bible, we can see that David's life has some similarities to Jesus' life. The first similarity is that they were both born in Bethlehem. Also, David's family line ties to Jesus. That makes David an ancestor of Jesus born about 1,000 years prior to Jesus' birth.

Another similarity is that David was a shepherd and Jesus is also known as the Good Shepherd, caring for us as His sheep. Also, David was a servant and Jesus is also known as the Servant King. David defeated Goliath, and Jesus defeated Satan. Similarly, David ruled on an earthly throne and Jesus reigns on the Heavenly throne.

It is so splendid to see prophecy being fulfilled in the Bible. In this case, the Messiah was to come from the root or seed of David, and Jesus did. Joseph, Jesus's earthly father, was from the tribe of Judah. Mary, His mother was also of the lineage of David. Jesus is considered the root of David.

In the 22nd chapter of Psalms, we read the prophecy that David wrote concerning Jesus. Psalm 22 is referred to as "Psalm of the Cross" because it portrays Christ on the cross. David was inspired by the Holy Spirit and prophesies of Jesus' death and resurrection more than 1,000 years before it even happened.

Let's compare David's prophecy to the gospel's description of Jesus' death and see the similarities. In Psalm 22:18, David writes,

"They divide my garments among them, and for my clothing they cast lots."

We read in the New Testament what Matthew, Mark, Luke and John all share about Jesus' crucifixion in correlation to what David's writes in the Old Testament.

Matthew 27:35
"And they had crucified him, and divided his garments among them by casting lots."

Mark 15:24
"And they crucified him and divided his garments among them, casting lots for them, to decide what each should take."

Luke 23:34
"And Jesus said, "Father, forgive them, for they know not what they do." And they cast lots to divide his garments."

John 19:23
"When the soldiers had crucified Jesus, they took his garments and divided them into four parts, one part for each soldier; also his tunic."

And in Psalm 22:1-2, David said,

"My God, my God, why have you forsaken me? Why are you so far from saving me, from the words of my groaning? O my God, I

cry by day, but you do not answer, and by night, I find no rest."

And then we compare what David said to what Matthew said in Matthew 27:45-46,

"Now from the sixth hour there was darkness over all the land until the ninth hour. And about the ninth hour Jesus cried out with a loud voice, saying, "Eli, Eli, lama sabachthani?" that is "My God, my God, why have you forsaken me?"

And then Mark witnesses the same that Matthew did in Mark 15:34,

"And at the ninth hour Jesus cried with a loud voice, "Eloi, Eloi, lama sabachthani? which means, My God, my God, why hast thou forsaken me?"

These verses are just some of the similarities and comparisons between David's prophecy in the Old Testament versus what the disciples wrote of Jesus's death on the cross in the New Testament.

As you read Psalm 22, you can feel what Jesus experienced on the cross through the words of David so many years before it actually happened.

Another song I wrote comes to mind here. It's about Jesus and his death and resurrection and it's entitled, *"Hallelujah."* The lyrics are as follows:

"Hallelujah"

On the cross of Calvary,
Was the one who died for me;
Lamb of God, Lord of Lords, The Risen King.
From the cross your mercy flowed,
Making me white as the snow;
All of my sin was washed away, I'm free.

Hallelujah! Hallelujah!
To the One who died for me.
Hallelujah! Hallelujah!
To the One who set me free.

Now I sing a brand-new song,
In my heart, all day long;
To the name above all names, Jesus.
For all that He has done for me,
More and more I clearly see,
How His love comforts and takes care of me.

Hallelujah! Hallelujah!
To the One who died for me.
Hallelujah! Hallelujah!
To the One who set me free.

I can hear the angels sing,
Hallelujah to the King;
Around the throne adoring Him, Unto the Lamb.
Holy, Holy being sung;
Jesus Christ the Living One,
Kings of Kings, Lord of Lords, Saviour.

Hallelujah! Hallelujah!
To the One who died for me.
Hallelujah! Hallelujah!
To the One who set me free.
Jodi Warren ©2017

Right after the prophetic words in Psalm 22, we get to read Psalm 23, where David writes, "The Lord is my Shepherd, I shall not want." Nothing is by coincidence. Jesus was, and is, and is to come. He is the Good Shepherd. He is the Alpha and Omega, the beginning and the end. God's word is everlasting. As David says in Psalm 90:2,

"Before the mountains were brought forth, or
ever thou had formed the earth and the world,
from everlasting to everlasting, you are God."

It is impossible for David to have known what would take place 1,000 plus years later, but God did and this is why we have these beautiful truths and these beautiful life lessons that we see in the life of David.

Behold, the Lamb of God,
who takes away
the sin of the world.

Chapter 14

Obedience to God and His Ways

And all these blessing shall come upon you
and overtake you, if you obey the
voice of the Lord your God.

Deuteronomy 5:22

David continuously tried to do what was right in the eyes of God all the days of his life. We read this in 1 Kings 15:5,

> *"Because David did that which was right in the eyes of the Lord and did not turn aside from anything that he commanded him all the days of his life, except in the matter of Uriah the Hittite."*

What an accomplishment. However, I want you to notice one phrase of that verse, "except for the matter of Uriah the Hittite," referring to his sin, the distraction as was mentioned earlier. I'm sure David would've rather that verse not have included that painful truth, so I'm going to give us a reminder to not be distracted when it comes to serving the Lord and being a person after God's heart. When we stand before Him, we want Him to say, "Well done my good and faithful servant, enter in." Draw a line in the sand and say, no more distractions. It's all for the Lord.

Now, we look at the prophet Samuel's view of obedience to God's ways and commands from what he speaks to Saul. We read in 1 Samuel 15:22,

> *"Behold, to obey is better than sacrifice, and to listen than the fat of rams."*

Samuel said this to King Saul because Saul was preforming outward rituals, rather than following God's commands. God wants your life. He wants you to talk to him. He wants your heart to be directed to Him. He wants true repentance. He doesn't just want to hear you or see you on Sunday morning at the local church. He wants you obeying and seeking Him right where you are each day. In Psalm 40:6-8, David states that God does not delight in sacrifice, but He delights in obedience.

> *"In sacrifice and offering you have not delighted, but you have given me an open ear. Burnt offering and sin offering you have not required. Then I said, 'Behold I have come; in the scroll of the book it is written of me: I will delight to do your will, O my God; your law is within my heart.'"*

We learn from the prophet Samuel and King David that it is better to obey God. God doesn't want that ram of sacrifice, or in today's words, that twenty-dollar bill in the offering plate. He wants you to obey His voice and obey His commands and statues. Going to church, sacrificing of your time, giving of your money is needed and it's well and good, but when everything is all said and done, all the Lord really wants is all of you.

When you read the end of the verse above in Psalm 40:8, David writes,

> *"I delight to do your will, O my God; your law is within my heart."*

Delight to do God's will, that is obedience. David constantly obeyed the Lord. He put his trust in the Lord. In Psalm 56:3-4 we read,

> *"When I am afraid, I put my trust in you. In God, whose word I praise, in God I trust; I shall not be afraid. What can flesh do to me?"*

I'm finding as we strive to be Christians, and people after God's heart, that one thing leads to another. Humility leads to belief, faith leads to being filled with the Spirit, trust leads to obedience, and gratitude leads to loving the Lord with all your heart.

I am reminded of another song that I wrote years ago entitled, *"I Will Follow"* and the words are as follows:

"I WILL FOLLOW"

Now and for always,
For all of my life;
I will follow.
Through the good
and even the bad,
The happy the sad,
I will follow.

For Your ways are not my ways,
And your thoughts
much higher than mine;
much higher than mine.

I will follow you, whatever the cost,
I will follow.
And Your ways will be my ways,
I will stand,
I will follow You.

Here, I make this vow,
Right here and right now;
I will follow.
And My feet
will walk like the deer;
You are my shield,
I will follow.

For Your ways are not my ways,
And your thoughts
much higher than mine;
much higher than mine.

I will not be afraid,
I will be strong and brave!

I will follow you, whatever the cost,
I will follow.
And Your ways will be my ways,
I will stand,
I will follow You.

Jodi Warren ©2017

I pray as you read the words of this song, that it becomes not only words to you, but also a prayer that you pray in your heart.

It states in Isaiah 55:8-9 that Gods ways are not our ways, his thoughts are higher than ours,

> *"For my thoughts are not your thoughts, neither are your ways my ways saith the Lord. For as the heavens are higher than the earth so are my ways higher than yours and my thoughts than your thoughts."*

David was a man after God's heart because he trusted God and God's strength rather than his own strength. He knew Gods ways were the right ways. David always strived to do what was right in the eyes of God. His delight was to follow the ways of the Lord.

Conclusion

In reading this book, I hope the words you have read speak to your heart. You are good enough! Do not hesitate to do what God puts on your heart. Little things lead to big things. God's timing is the best timing. God's ways are the best ways.

There are different seasons of life. I've had this book on my heart for many years now. The thought was there, but it wasn't the time, it wasn't the season. But now the season has arrived. I don't know what season you are in, but take in whatever this season holds for you.

I find it amazing how each spring the daffodils always come up, and in the summer, the black-eyed Susan's always just seem to appear. They are all tucked away, nestled in the ground until it's the right season for them to thrive.

Let us learn from the life of David and strive to have a heart after God.

Be strong and courageous!
Do all that God puts on your heart.
Little David, play your harp.

The songs read in the course of this book are on the EP entitled, "Little David, Play Your Harp" by Jodi Warren and are currently streaming on Spotify, Amazon Music, iTunes, YouTube, and other streaming sites, and can also be found on Amazon.

I would encourage you to pause your reading when you come upon a song within the book, listen to the music, and meditate upon the message.

May God bless you on your journey as you grow closer to Him.